Fagan Around is a blog of many different genres. It is pictures. It is politics. It is random reposts of things the blogger that runs the site, Ryan Fagan, finds interesting, funny, or dumb. Within these pages you will find a "best of" covering the best posts from the site's first 283 posts, ranging in date from May 13, 2013 – November 29, 2013. Enjoy! Oh, and visit www.faganaround.com for the latest posts AND for posts that are not featured here!

Enjoy!

פייגן ריאן

The post that started it all:

HURRAH MINNESOTA!

May 13, 2013

(Photo Credit: St Paul Pioneer Press: Ben Garvin)

Congrats to Minnesota for becoming the first Midwestern state to get themselves onto the right side of history!!! I wish was there to celebrate with my friends, both gay and straight! People on both sides of the aisle supporting the right for consenting adults to have the legal recognition of a marriage. I am a Catholic but I am also a liberal with an open mind that can read between the lines enough to know that "marriage" was not invented by Christians. It has been around since before the time that Jesus walked the earth. I think many anti-gay marriage people may be wrapping up the sacrament of "holy matrimony" too much into the general, legal "marriage" thing. If churches, mosques, or synagogues don't want to perform the legal joining of two consenting guys or two consenting girls, they don't have to... But if two guys or two girls want to go down to the courthouse, get a marriage license (for those of you following at home, that is the legal, non religious document we all have to get before we get married), and have a justice of the peace legally marry them, they should be allowed that right.

One thing that's become obvious over the course of the debate is how little many people understand about civics.

This entire issue has been about Civil Marriage. Not Religious Marriage. There is a confusing overlap but the difference is plain and clear to anyone who pays attention. People have been intentionally blurring these two very different concepts together. The Government has never tried to make the Catholic Church marry non-Catholics, or divorced people, and nobody has ever said a word about that. Nor should they.

This is about the dignity of being able to have the legal contract that you get from the government that you sign so that two people of the same sex that are in a loving and committed relationship can have the same rights together through life and end of life. For it or against it, the fact is this:

The act of two people of the same sex joining together in the legal state of marriage doesn't affect ANYONE else in the world in any way, shape, or form.

Its. The. Law.

May 16, 2013

Deal. With. It.

#ObamaCareInThreeWords

Premium McWrap: A Review

May 18, 2013

Recently I was awarded a [Klout](#) Perk that was a $5 McDonald's gift card. With this gift card I was to go down to one of my 250 (slight exaggeration) local McDonald's locations and try one of the new Premium McWraps. I decided to head over today to the McDonald's located about one block from my apartment and try the Chicken and Ranch one... With grilled chicken, of course.

As you can see above, there are three Premium McWraps to choose from. All three can have crispy or grilled chicken.
1. Chicken and Bacon
2. Sweet Chili Chicken
3. Chicken and Ranch

As I said before, I chose Chicken and Ranch... I like chicken. I like ranch. It made perfect damn sense then, now didn't it?

I was happy to see that it really is a decent sized wrap. Whenever I have seen a commercial I thought that McDonald's was using the magic of television to make it look big but then in actuality I would get one sometime and see that it was only slightly larger than a Snack Wrap.

Nope. The actual product matches what you see on television.

Now, as for the full ingredient specs, we have grilled chicken breast filet with two half slices of tomato, cucumber slices, spring greens, shredded lettuce and cheddar jack cheese, all drizzled with seasoned rice vinegar and buttermilk ranch sauce wrapped in a flour tortilla. It was impressive for McDonald's.

It was a mouthful (THAT'S WHAT SHE SAID). It really was tasty. I would get it again. I recommend trying it. Not bad. Well done McDonald's. You now have a product that I could see on an Applebee's menu. Now, I said Applebee's... Lets take that as a compliment in this instance, ok!?

CLIMATE CHANGE: HOW MUCH MORE PROOF DO DENIERS NEED?

May 20, 2013

It has always boggled my mind that climate change is even a political debate topic. How can anyone deny or lack the belief that it is happening? Extreme weather, melting ice caps, and yo-yo temperature changes are just a few of the obvious things that prove it is real. It is ridiculous to debate this.

I remember when I was in elementary school (1988-1993) we were being told about global warming and how it was a real threat to the planet and when I turned on the television at home I wasn't being told it was not real… Recycling and planting trees and lowering emissions were all things that were heralded and encouraged. Now, twenty-plus years later, with the science and theories practically proven and stronger than ever, it is debated by people and some think it is some 'liberal myth' and that is ridiculous. Fox News treats it like the "Creationism vs Evolution" debate. Ridiculous.

Climate change deniers need to pull their heads out of their asses before it is too late.

Update – 5/20/13 @ 1:09pm: Minnesota State Rep Glenn Gruenhagen (R-Glencoe) thinks climate change is a "complete United Nations fraud and lie"
http://thinkprogress.org/climate/2013/05/19/2031191/mn-state-rep-climate-change-united-nations-fraud-and-lie/?mobile=nc

Wow, Minnesota has some regions that really know how to pick representatives. (Sarcasm)

Update – 5/20/13 @ 2:43pm: Sarah Palin is still a tool... and a blind fool.
http://www.huffingtonpost.com/2013/05/20/sarah-palin-global-warming_n_3306867.html

She Wants The D

May 21, 2013

Oh, CNN, you did a great job picking a bro to interview after the Oklahoma tornado yesterday. In this guy's defense, maybe it was the only shirt he could find in the rubble? No, the more likely scenario is that he was working out at an area Gold's Gym and saw the news van approaching and then raced to help victims so he could see the reporters and tell his story.

Franken Has Lead Over All Potential Opponents

May 21, 2013

I met and had my picture taken with Al Franken during a campaign stop in St Cloud, Minnesota. June 2008

As someond who voted for him in 2008 while I lived in Minnesota, I was happy to hear that Minnesota U.S. Sen. Al Franken leads all potential GOP opponents by comfortable double-digit margins, according to a Public Policy Polling survey released Tuesday. Among those tested by the Democratic polling firm was U.S. Rep. Michele Bachmann, who he leads 55-38, a 17 point margin. Franken leads conservative talk show host Jason Lewis by the same 17 point margin (54-37), as well as state Sen. Julianne Ortman (52-35).

Narrowing the gap slightly against the first-term senator were businessman Mike McFadden and Hennepin County Sheriff Rich Stanek, who came within 15 points apiece (both at 51-36). Sen. Julie Rosen trailed by 16 points (52-36). Overall, Franken weighed in with a 51 percent approval rating.

Shine Bright

May 23, 2013

Great Waters Brewing Company

May 28, 2013

Saturday evening, my wife and I had dinner at <u>Great Waters Brewing Company</u> at 426 Saint Peter Street in St Paul. It was a place I had heard of and have always wanted to try, due to it being a brewpub and all...

At each table they have a "Beer Key" printed out that shows all the current Great Waters beer on tap and the specs of each beer. I think that is really cool.

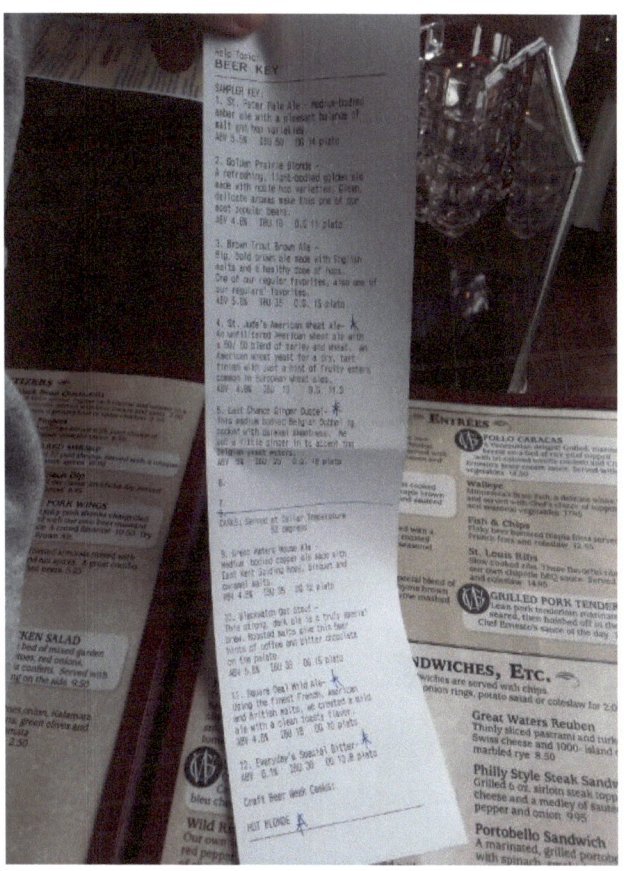

Nice view from our table looking out onto Saint Peter Street.

They have a nice patio area but it was a bit cold to eat outside Saturday evening.

Delicious brewed beer

Bye Bye Bachmann

May 29, 2013

top news

Bachmann announces she won't seek re-election

In an early morning video, Michele Bachmann said she won't run again in 2014. The high-profile congresswoman had a narrow re-election last year and is under investigation for her 2012 presidential campaign.

Wow. This is a headline to behold! Bat $hit Crazy Bachmann spends millions on a television ad buy an unprecedented 18 months before the election and then calls it a day 2 weeks later. She said her prospects for being re-elected and the investigations into her former presidential campaign had no impact on her decision... Yeah. Right. Say whatever you want Michele, but I think most people outside your base are intelligent enough to read through that and see that you are scared.

Bachmann didn't give a formal reason for retiring, except to say that she considered four terms in the U.S. House of Representatives enough. Even though there aren't term limits for members of Congress, she said, presidents are only allowed to serve for eight years, and, "in my opinion, well, eight years is also long enough an individual to serve as representative for a specific congressional district."

Though Bachmann is a favorite among conservatives and Tea Party groups, she underperformed with the electorate at large, relative to the solidly conservative 6th District. Mitt Romney won the district by more than 15 percent in 2012, while Bachmann won by just 1.3 percent. Last week, the Jim Graves campaign released an internal poll showing a statistically-tied race between the two.

Bachmann did not say what she'll do after retiring from the House... Probably something on the Fox News payroll. Unfortunately, she didn't rule out a return to politics in the future.

The Eight Most Outlandish Moments of Bachmann's Congressional Career

May 29, 2013

As we celebrate the big news that Michele Bachmann is not seeking reelection in 2014, here is a list of some of Michele Bachmann's most controversial moments in congress:

1. Bachmann peddled a dangerous anti-vaccine conspiracy. Bachmann pushed the disproved theory that the vaccine for HPV — which prevents cervical cancer — can cause mental retardation. That misinformation has had a wide and lasting impact: Vaccination rates are still remarkably low, and experts blame figureheads like Bachmann who communicated misleading information to the public.

2. Bachmann called being gay 'personal enslavement.' On the issue of LGBT rights, Bachmann has a long record of either mocking gay and trans (like when she said she'd mistaken ex-gay therapy for anti-aging therapy, 'pray away the grey'). But when she isn't mocking sexual orientation, she has treated it more like a mental disorder. Famously, Bachmann once said, "It's a very sad life. It's part of Satan, I think, to say this is gay. It's anything but gay. [...] Because if you're involved in the gay and lesbian lifestyle, it's bondage. Personal bondage, personal despair, and personal enslavement. And that's why this is so dangerous."

3. Bachmann considers climate change 'a hoax.' While experts warn that global climate change is already set to have a lasting impact on our environment, Bachmann calls climate change "all voodoo, nonsense, hokum, a hoax." She also cast doubt on the entire field of climate science. At a town hall in her district, Bachmann informed constituents that climate science is not "real science" but "manufactured science."

4. Bachmann led an Islamophobic witch hunt. Last year, Bachmann sought to "expose" members of the Muslim Brotherhood within the U.S. government. The totally unfounded witch hunt was essentially Bachmann's personal indictment of one of then-Sec. of State Hillary Clinton's aides, Huma Abedin, but it also served to fuel anti-Muslim bigotry. Bachmann's fellow party members came out against her, with Sen. John McCain (R-AZ) slamming her on the Senate floor for her "unwarranted and unfounded attack."

5. Bachmann claimed Obamacare would 'literally' kill people. In a screed against Obamacare on the House floor, Bachmann warned that the law "literally kills women, kills children, kills senior citizens." She also questioned, in an interview with a fringe website that peddles conspiracy theories, whether Obamacare would allow the IRS to "deny or delay access to health care" for conservatives.

6. Bachmann told the American people that Iran had plans to nuke the U.S. During a presidential debate on the issue of national security, Bachmann falsely claimed that Iranian

President Mahmoud Ahmadinejad had laid out plans to bomb the United States with a nuclear weapon.

7. Bachmann called on the American media to investigate 'anti-American' politicians. Bachmann's first witch hunt of her career was against her own colleagues in Congress. In 2008, Bachmann told MSNBC's Chris Matthews that she hoped the media would investigate Democratic members of Congress, including Rep. Nancy Pelosi (D-CA) and Sen. Harry Reid (D-NV). "I wish the American media would take a great look at the views of the people in Congress," she said, "and find out, are they pro-America or anti-America?"

8. Bachmann wanted to abolish the minimum wage to help job growth. Back at the start of her Congressional career, Bachmann told the Minnesota state Senate, "Literally, if we took away the minimum wage — if conceivably it was gone — we could potentially virtually wipe out unemployment completely because we would be able to offer jobs at whatever level."

List courtesy of Think Progress

10 of the Craziest Things Michele Bachmann Has Ever Said

May 29, 2013

Michele Bachmann

In keeping with today's general 'Michele Bachmann is Bat Shit Crazy' theme here at Fagan Around, I now share with you the 10 craziest things she has ever said, as compiled by ThinkProgress:

1. BACHMANN WARNED 'THE LION KING' WAS GAY PROPAGANDA: At the November 2004 EdWatch National Education Conference, Bachmann said the "normalization" of homosexuality would lead to "desensitization": "Very effective way to do this with a bunch of second graders, is take a picture of 'The Lion King' for instance, and a teacher might say, 'Do you know that the music for this movie was written by a gay man?' The message is: I'm better at what I do, because I'm gay."

2. BACHMANN CLAIMED ABOLISHING THE MINIMUM WAGE WOULD CREATE JOBS: While testifying in front of the Minnesota Senate in 2005, Bachmann said, "Literally, if we took away the minimum wage — if conceivably it was gone — we could potentially virtually wipe out unemployment completely because we would be able to offer jobs at whatever level." This isn't remotely true. Even simply reducing the minimum wage would, as Paul Krugman noted, "at best do nothing for employment; more likely it would actually be contractionary."

3. BACHMANN CLAIMED THAT SCIENTISTS ARE SUPPORTERS OF INTELLIGENT DESIGN: During a 2006 debate, Bachmann said, "There are hundreds and hundreds of scientists, many of them holding Nobel Prizes, who believe in intelligent design." This was, and is, not true.

4. BACHMANN CLAIMED TERRI SCHIAVO WAS 'HEALTHY': Not long after Terri Schiavo died, Bachmann said she would have voted for the Palm Sunday Compromise because Schiavo "was healthy. She had brain damage — there was brain damage, there was no question. But from a health point of view, she was not terminally ill." An autopsy found that Schiavo had suffered irreversible brain damage and her brain, said the medical examiner, was "profoundly atrophied."

5. BACHMANN LIKENED VISITING IRAQ TO VISITING MALL OF AMERICA: In 2007, Bachmann returned from a junket to Iraq and told her colleagues, "[T]here's a commonality with the Mall of America, in that it's on that proportion. There's marble everywhere. The other thing I remarked about was there is water everywhere." As ThinkProgress documented at the time, the comparison was preposterous.

6. BACHMANN CLAIMED THAT CARBON DIOXIDE IS 'HARMLESS': In 2008, a Stanford scientist revealed "direct links" between increased levels of carbon dioxide in the atmosphere and "increases in human mortality" — globally, he found that as many as "20,000 air-pollution-related deaths per year per degree Celsius may be due to this greenhouse gas." The next year, Bachmann, who is not a scientist, said that "carbon dioxide is portrayed as harmful. But there isn't even one study that can be produced that shows that carbon dioxide is a harmful gas."

7. BACHMANN CALLED FOR A CONGRESSIONAL WITCH HUNT: Pivoting off the news of Barack Obama's alleged relationship to former Weather Underground member William Ayers, and his former pastor, Rev. Jeremiah Wright, Bachmann accused the candidate of having "anti-American views." She then suggested that Congressional liberals — including Nancy Pelosi and Harry Reid — ought to be subject to "an exposé" by the media because of their views. "I think people would love to see like that," she told a stunned Chris Matthews.

8. BACHMANN SUGGESTED GAY SINGER SHOULD REPENT AFTER GETTING CANCER: Bachmann saw Melissa Etheridge's cancer as a teachable moment: "Unfortunately she is now suffering from breast cancer, so keep her in your prayers," she said in November 2004. "This may be an opportunity for her now to be open to some spiritual things, now that she is suffering with that physical disease. She is a lesbian."

9. BACHMANN BOASTED ABOUT BREAKING THE LAW: In advance of the 2010 national Census, Bachmann told The Washington Times that she would break the law by not completing the forms. "I know for my family, the only question we will be answering is how many people are in our home," she said. "We won't be answering any information beyond that, because the Constitution doesn't require any information beyond that."

10. BACHMANN CLAIMED THAT GLENN BECK COULD SOLVE THE DEBT CRISIS: During a February trip to South Carolina, Bachmann told a South Carolina audience, "I think if we give Glenn Beck the numbers, he can solve this [the national debt]."

Traditional Marriage

May 29, 2013

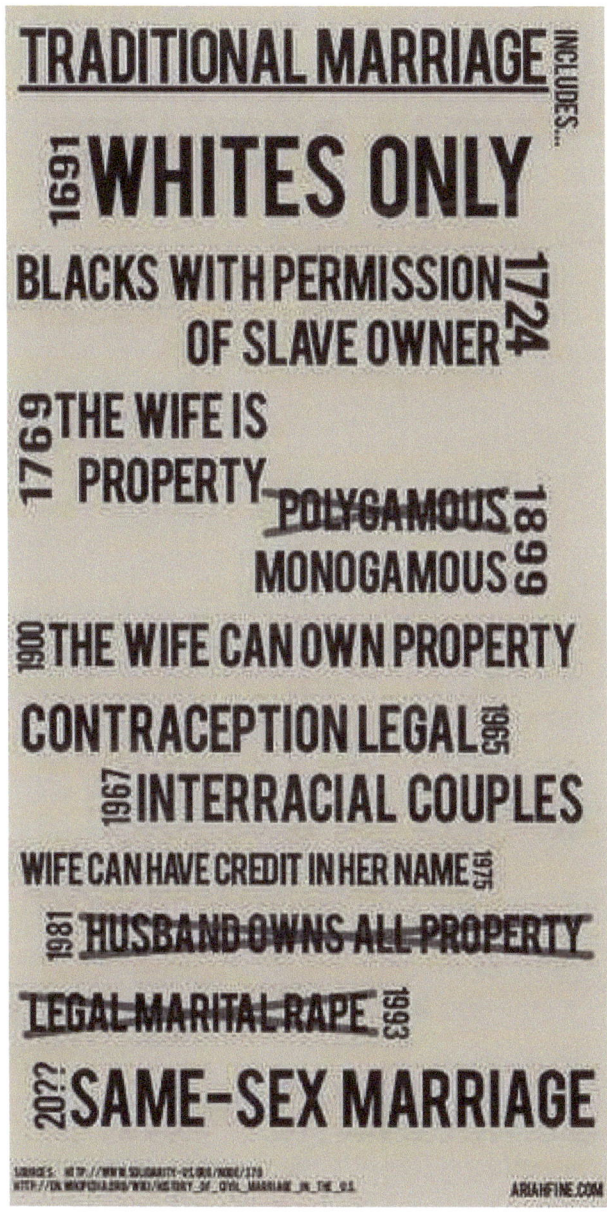

We have been "redefining marriage" for centuries... Equality is IMPORTANT. Why stop now?

How to Finally (Hopefully) Stop An Annoying Daily Call

June 4, 2013

This overseas call center keeps number spoofing my phone (illegal) and calling me even though I am on the no-call registry (illegal). They say they are calling for Howard Daniels and that my payday loan is pre-approved. First off, I am not Howard Daniels. I do not know a Howard Daniels. I have had the same phone number since May 2009. Second, I don't need a payday loan.

They call a dozen times an hour on some days. I tell them there is no Howard at my number, they either say "sorry" and hang up, or they just hang up. Oh, but then they call back 2 minutes later. Finally today I tried a new approach, which I later explained to my wife in an email in which the words of the caller are in quotes:

That payday loan place called for Howard Daniels again... I told them he died... "You're joking!!??"

No, he passed away 3 months ago...

"Who are you? His friend, his brother?"

His friend

"And you have his number since 3 months ago? "

Yes. Yes. They signed his cell phone contract over to me.

"That is so weird because he has payday loan with us and we have all his info and this number"

Yep. Yep. So, yeah, he is dead so you can stop calling.

It has been 20 minutes since I told the callers about Howard being deceased and they haven't called back again. Crap, I hope i didn't just jinx it.

THE Place to Get Your Nails Done In Minneapolis

June 5, 2013

Do Me Nails

Located on Lake Street

Top 3 Things Heard From Republican Trolls

June 9, 2013

The three things heard most often from Republican Trolls:

1.)"I'm not a Republican I'm an Independent"

2.)"I don't watch Fox News, I have my own sources"

3.)"I'm not the ignorant one"

I guess I can understand...If I were a Republican I'd deny it too...

The problem is, wrong wing trolls, that in denying your own party and its personal news outlet you've basically stated that you're embarrassed to admit that you vote for stupidity religiously...

Oh, and 99% of the time it is you who is ignorant...

A Few Things Created Entirely By Advertisers

June 11, 2013

Just a few of the things that were created entirely by advertisers: The Pledge of Allegiance (1892, to sell flags), the requirement of buying a diamond engagement ring (1938), Valentine's Day candy (1892), Father's Day (1908), Rudolph the Red Nosed Reindeer (1939, a Macy's holiday coloring book), wedding registries (1924), green bean casserole (1955), Santa Claus (at least in his modern incarnation, 1931), the need for most pharmaceuticals (began in the 70's: the lab creates the drug, but the ads create the "disease" which never existed before, i.e., creating the need for a drug that no one ever knew they needed), women shaving their legs and underarms (1915), and of course Christmas presents.

Wisconsin Needs A Governor Who...

June 12, 2013

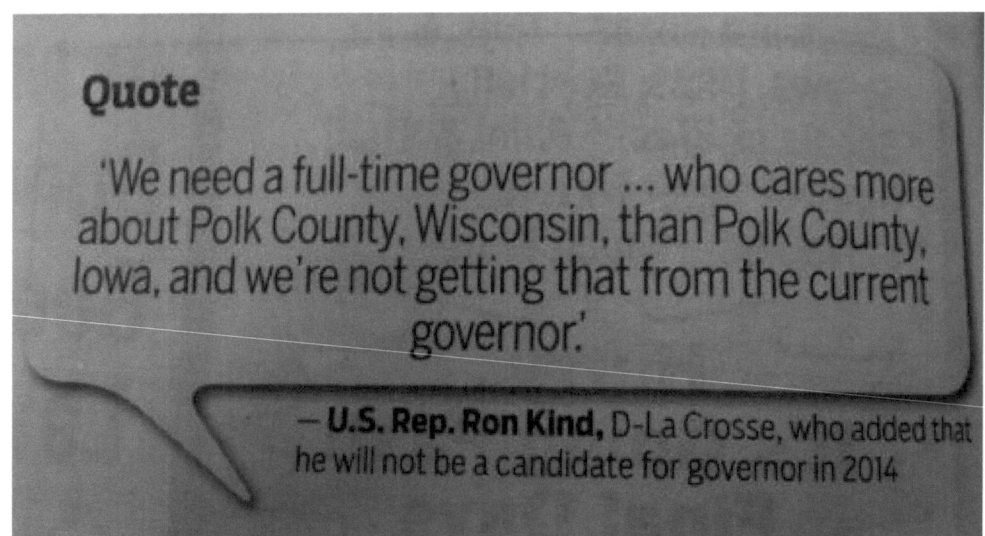

Quote

'We need a full-time governor ... who cares more about Polk County, Wisconsin, than Polk County, Iowa, and we're not getting that from the current governor.'

— **U.S. Rep. Ron Kind,** D-La Crosse, who added that he will not be a candidate for governor in 2014

Ten Political Things You Can't Do If You Are Following Jesus

June 12, 2013

Jesus didn't worry much about stepping on political toes, and the Bible insists that governments be just toward the least of these **(the books of the prophets alone make this point very clear)**. Frequently, people who are the most vocal about not making Jesus political are the same people who want prayer in school and laws based on their own religious perspectives. By a happy little circumstance that brings us to this list of the TEN POLITICAL THINGS YOU CAN'T DO IF YOU ARE FOLLOWING JESUS:

10) Force your religious beliefs and practices on others.

One of the strengths of the faith Jesus taught was in its meekness. The faith he taught valued free will over compulsion – because that's how love works. Compelling people to follow any religion, more or less your personal religion, stands over and against the way Jesus practiced his faith. If you are using the government to compel people to practice your spiritual beliefs, you might be the reason baby Jesus is crying. This does get tricky. There is a difference in letting your beliefs inform your political choices and letting your politics enforce your religion. This article is about the first part.

9) Advocate for war.

There's a reason why he was called the Prince of Peace. Sure, you can quote, "I did not come to bring peace, but a sword," and even two or three other verses, but they don't hold a candle to the more than fifty-some verses where Jesus speaks about peace and peacemaking. It's funny how things keep coming back to love but it needs to be said, it is way far away from loving a person to kill them. I guess there's a reason why we say, "God is love." In the end, love wins.

8) Favor the rich over the poor.

This is actually related to #4. Favoring the rich over the poor is a slap in the face of Jesus, his life, and his teachings. In terms of the teachings of Jesus, it is bad enough when we allow the rich to take advantage of the poor, but when we create laws that not only encourage the behavior but also protect it? Well, let's just say it becomes crystal clear how ironic it is that we print, "In God We Trust," on our money.

7) Cut funding that hurts the least of these.

To some degree, this is the inverse of #8. Favoring the rich is despicable. We Jesus minions should avoid it. Hurting the poor? Well, that's just … just … um, something a whole lot worse than despicable. Despicabler? Über-despicable? When Jesus said, "Whatever you do to the least of these, you do it to me," he meant it. When you cut funding and it hurts people, according to Jesus, you are hurting him.

6) Let people go hungry.

It is a political issue. Spiritually, Gandhi said, "There are people in the world so hungry, that God cannot appear to them except in the form of bread." Politically, hunger causes problems with education, production, and civil behavior that are all necessary for a successful nation. More importantly for Christians, Jesus said when we feed the hungry, we are feeding him. So, yes, this item is on both lists – and I'm going to do it again.

5) Withhold healthcare from people.

Did you ever play the game "Follow the Leader?" If you don't do what the leader does, you are out. Following means you should imitate as closely as possible. When people who were sick needed care, Jesus gave it to them. If we are following Jesus, we will imitate him as closely as possible. No, the government can't repeat the miracles he did but I've seen modern medicine do things that are about as close to a miracle as I expect to get. While the government can't do miracles, it can supply modern medicine. Every year, 45,000 people die in the U.S. because of the lack of healthcare. We Christians like to talk about "saving" people. Well, I know of about 45,000 people who'd love for us to do it and we should – because that's how love works.

4) Limit the rights of a select group of people.

Jesus loves everybody – but he loves me best. Kind of sits the wrong way with you, doesn't it? Well, it should and with good reason. If you spend any time reading the Bible you know that we all were made in God's image. Exactly which part of us is in God's image is less clear, but what is clear is that we were equally made in the image of God. Any law that doesn't treat people equally is as good as thumbing your nose at God. Even worse? Doing it in the name of God or based on religious beliefs (see #10).

3) Turn away immigrants.

Christian heritage runs through Judaism. We are an immigrant people. Even our religion began somewhere else. Our spiritual ancestors, Abraham and Sarah, were told by God to pick up what they had and start traveling. Moses, Miriam, and Aaron led a nation out of Egypt, into the desert and ultimately to new lands. Even Jesus spent part of his childhood as a foreigner in a foreign land. As Exodus says, we know how it feels to be foreigners in a foreign land. If you don't think being foreigners in a foreign land is still our story, ask the Native Americans. At best, turning away immigrants makes us hypocrites; at worst, it makes us betrayers of our ancestors and our God.

2) Devalue education.

We learn in Proverbs that wisdom is something in which God delights daily. As a matter of fact, according to Proverbs, wisdom is better than gold. When you look at the percentage of our budget that goes to education and at what Congress is trying to do to student loans, it's pretty clear that delighting in wisdom is something our government no longer does.

1) Support capital punishment — execution.

Jesus died by execution. He was an innocent man. Every year, innocent people die by execution in our nation. It's time to be a shining city on a hill. It's time to express the fullness of love, to express the value of life. It's time to stop the government-sanctioned killing.

How To Tweet Congressman Sean Duffy

June 13, 2013

Today, I sent tweets to all the US House members from Wisconsin to tell them to vote to keep student loan rates down. I made sure to add a bit more to my tweet to the representative of Wisconsin's 7th District, Sean Duffy.

Congressman Sean Duffy (R-WI)

Why? Well, I may not agree with him politically on pretty much anything... but I liked him on The Real World: Boston back in '97

Ryan Fagan @msnguy81   31s

@RepSeanDuffy I liked u on The Real World.
Also, please don't let student loan interest
rates double! #DreamsNotDebt
#DontDoubleMyRate

via Tweet Button

From the synopsis of the Boston season provided by MTV:
"Sean is a conservative Republican and an aspiring lawyer who competes in lumberjack competitions. He often clashes with the liberal-minded Kameelah. He later says he feels for Genesis because she is so hard on herself."

Congressman Duffy is the second from the left

I Agree

June 25, 2013

> To most Christians, the bible is like a software license. Nobody actually reads it. They just scroll to the bottom and click "I agree."

"Redefining" Is Not A New Thing

June 27, 2013

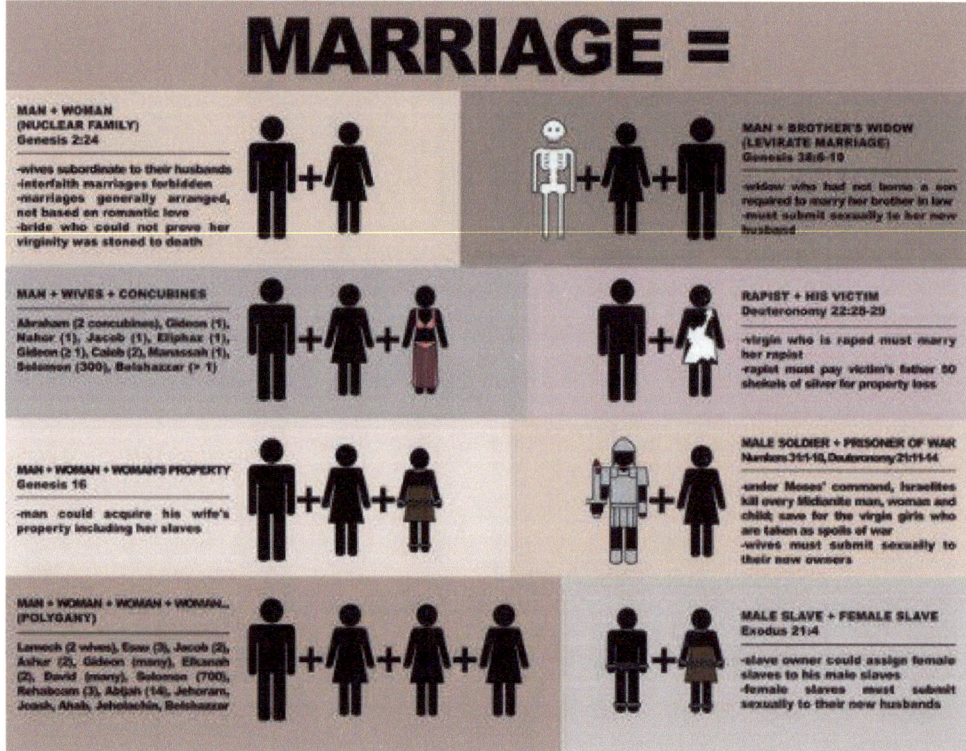

While it is a fact that marriage was not invented by Christians, Christians have been redefining it for centuries... I mean, look at the chart. The bible had many definitions.

If Catholics Can Live With Divorce, They Should Accept Gay Marriage Too

July 1, 2013

Andrew Sullivan, founding editor of The Dish, stopped by Fareed Zakaria's Global Public Square on CNN Sunday night and offered up an argument for why Catholics should accept gay marriage.

Sullivan, himself a practicing Catholic and an openly gay, married man, said that the biblical evidence that people use to oppose gay marriage has been misinterpreted, and that because Catholics accept divorce they should be willing to accept gay marriage as well.

"I would say the religious arguments are more based in fear than in the actual teachings, that they're based upon stray texts that actually don't mean what you think they mean and that Jesus himself *only said one thing about marriage*, which is that you can't divorce," he said. "And we live in a country where countless people are divorced. And that doesn't seem to threaten the religious liberty of Catholics. And it's as fundamental an issue."

"If Catholics can live with religious liberty with divorced people, they should be perfectly able to live with gay people, I mean, as married, as a civil marriage," Sullivan said.

25 Quotes From The Founders That Will Enrage The Tea Party

July 5, 2013

I love how Tea Baggers lay claim to the Founders. They can't stop themselves from insisting that the men who created this country through revolution, evolution and our Constitution would side with them in all things. Founders probably wouldn't find too much in common with a bunch of people who don't embrace education, science or progress and instead hold true to antiquated views and theocratic nonsense. So here are you can pull out the next time your great-uncle gets drunk at your family's Fourth of July barbecue and starts spouting off about how George Washington would hate modern America:

#25. "If ye love wealth better than liberty, the tranquility of servitude than the animated contest of freedom, go from us in peace." Samuel Adams

#24. "A nation under a well-regulated government, should permit none to remain uninstructed. It is monarchical and aristocratical government only that requires ignorance for its support." –Thomas Paine

#23. "Each individual of the society has a right to be protected by it in the enjoyment of his life, liberty, and property...He is obliged, consequently, to contribute his share to the expense of this protection; and to give his personal service, or an equivalent, when necessary." — John Adams

#22. "Educate and inform the whole mass of the people." — Thomas Jefferson

#21. "A government ought to contain in itself every power requisite to the full accomplishment of the objects committed to its care, and to the complete execution of the trusts for which it is responsible." –Alexander Hamilton

#20. "Believing with you that religion is a matter which lies solely between man and his God, that he owes account to none other for his faith or his worship...I contemplate with sovereign reverence that act of the whole American people which declared that their legislature should "make no law respecting an establishment of religion, or prohibiting the free exercise thereof," thus building a wall of separation between church and State." — Thomas Jefferson

#19. "...the right to freedom being the gift of God Almighty, it is not in the power of Man to alienate this gift, and voluntarily become a slave." –John Adams

#18. "Rights are not gifts from one man to another, nor from one class of men to another. It is impossible to discover any origin of rights otherwise than in the origin of man; it consequently follows that rights appertain to man in right of his existence, and must therefore be equal to every man." — Thomas Paine

#17. "The general spread of the light of science has already laid open to every view the palpable truth, that the mass of mankind has not been born with saddles on their backs, nor a favored few booted and spurred, ready to ride legitimately, by the grace of God." — Thomas Jefferson

#16. "Human government is more or less perfect as it approaches nearer or diverges farther from the imitation of this perfect plan of divine and moral government." –John Adams

#15. "Knowledge will forever govern ignorance: And a people who mean to be their own Governors, must arm themselves with the power which knowledge gives." — James Madison

#14. "As riches increase and accumulate in few hands, as luxury prevails in society, virtue will be in a greater degree considered as only a graceful appendage of wealth, and the tendency of things will be to depart from the republican standard." — Alexander Hamilton

#13. "My sons ought to study mathematics and philosophy, geography, natural history and naval architecture, navigation, commerce and agriculture, in order to give their children a right to study painting, poetry, music, architecture, statuary, tapestry, and porcelain." — John Adams

#12. "...to step into the field of Consumption, and tax special articles in that, as broadcloth or homespun, wine or whiskey, a coach or a wagon, is doubly taxing the same article. ...it is an aggrievance on the citizens who use these articles in exoneration of those who do not, contrary to the most sacred of the duties of a government, to do equal and impartial justice to all its citizens." — Thomas Jefferson

#11. "Equal laws protecting equal rights â€" the best guarantee of loyalty and love of country." –James Madison

#10. "Facts are stubborn things; and whatever may be our wishes, our inclination, or the dictates of our passions, they cannot alter the state of facts and evidence." –John Adams

#9. "...the minority possess their equal rights, which equal law must protect, and to violate would be oppression." — Thomas Jefferson

#8. "Born in other countries, yet believing you could be happy in this, our laws acknowledge, as they should do, your right to join us in society, conforming, as I doubt not you will do, to our established rules." –Thomas Jefferson

#7. "Every post is honorable in which a man can serve his country." — George Washington

#6. "We look forward to the time when the power to love will replace the love of power. Then will our world know the blessings of peace." –William Ellery

#5. "Question with boldness even the existence of a God; because if there be one he must approve of the homage of reason, than that of blindfolded fear." — Thomas Jefferson

#4. "Government is instituted for the common good; for the protection, safety, prosperity, and happiness of the people; and not for profit, honor, or private interest of any one man, family, or class of men..." –John Adams

#3. "He that would make his own liberty secure, must guard even his enemy from oppression; for if he violates this duty, he establishes a precedent that will reach to himself." –Thomas Paine

#2. "America united with a handful of troops, or without a single soldier, exhibits a more forbidding posture to foreign ambition than America disunited, with a hundred thousand veterans ready for combat." –James Madison

#1. "Equal and exact justice to all men, of whatever persuasion, religious or political." — Thomas Jefferson

The Original Famous Dave's

July 8, 2013

This weekend while visiting my family that was staying in a Hayward, Wisconsin area cabin, I was able to eat at the original [Famous Dave's BBQ](#) location. This location, which is located at the Grand Pines Resort, has a menu that is not entirely the same as the menu's at the rest of the chain's locations, giving it a more "local" feel than the cookie cutter nature of the other 100+ locations.

The view from my table looking outside at Round Lake

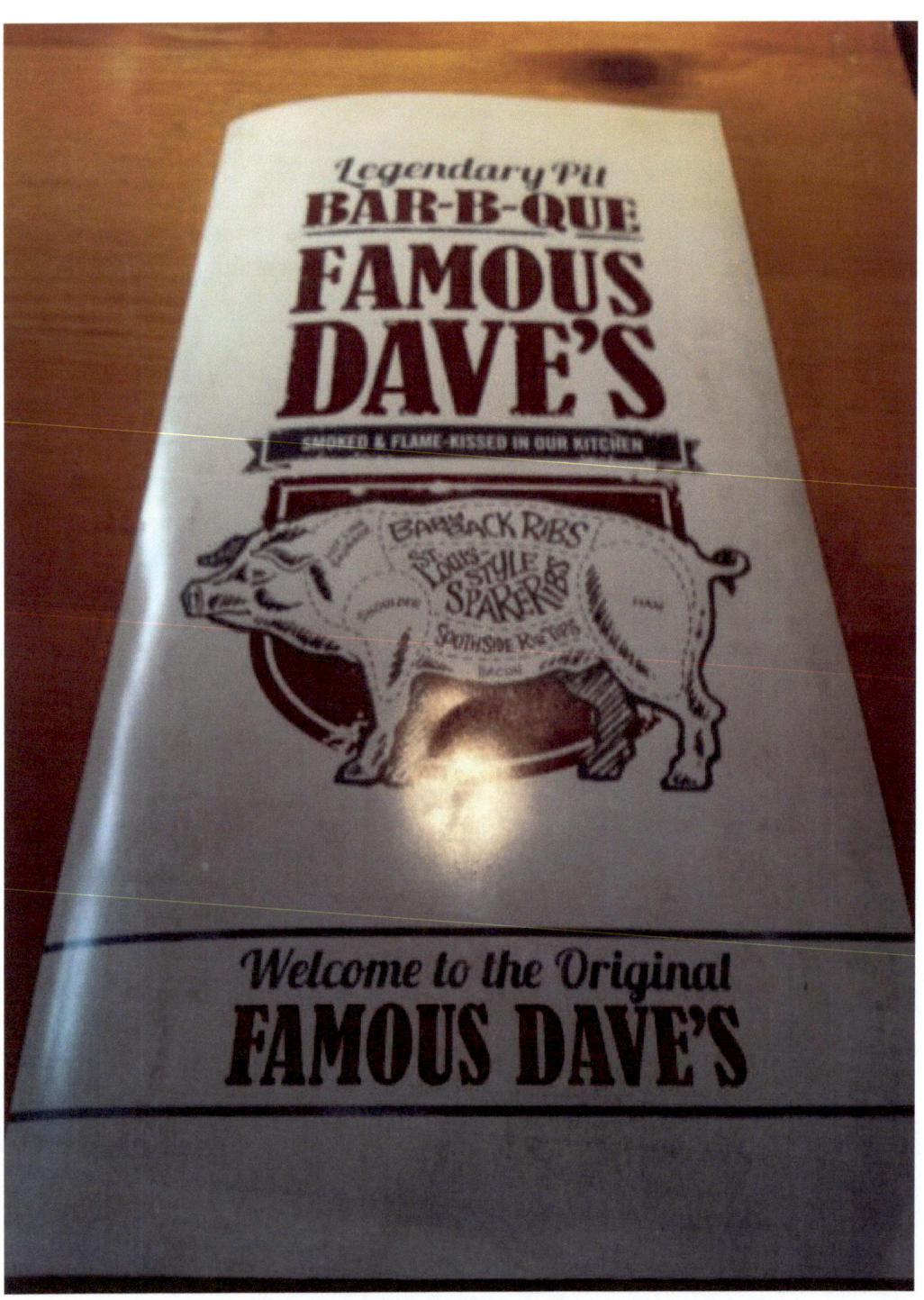

The menu

The bar area inside the restaurant

View looking out the other windows by my table

The outside patio seating area overlooks Round Lake

Mitt, Still Unable To Let It Go, Begins Campaigning In Africa

July 11, 2013

Shirts are distributed to campaign staffers at Mitt Romney's newly opened campaign office in Kenya

Ok, I kid... The shirts that were not purchased by supporters were sent to Africa to clothe people in need. One honorable thing we can say about his campaign...

The Most Thought-Provoking Excerpts From Chris Kluwe's Book

July 16, 2013

If you're familiar with Chris Kluwe's opinionated, profanity-strewn internet pieces, you have a pretty good idea what his book is like. *Beautifully Unique Sparkleponies* is a glorious mishmash of essays, letters, articles, and thoughts collected by the outspoken punter. Here are a few of the highlights in my opinion

So I forced myself to read *Atlas Shrugged*. Apparently I harbor masochistic tendencies; it was a long, hard slog, and by the end I felt as if Ayn Rand had violently beaten me about the head and shoulders with words. I feel I would be doing all of you a disservice (especially those who think Rand is really super-duper awesome) if I didn't share some thoughts on this weighty tome.

cum-gargling shitmilitias immediately start attacking anyone who even hints that stricter gun control might not be such a bad idea. "ERMAGERD, IF THEY TAKE ERR GUNZ WE CAN'T FIGHT THE FEDARALIS WHEN THEY INVADE THE COMPOUND!! SLIPPERY SLOPE!! SECOND 'MEND-MENT!! SECOND 'MENDMENT!!"

Step 1. Connect to the Internet. If you're logging on through AOL's thirty-day free trial CD, please, for the love of all that's holy, do not try to Win the Internet. I promise you that it won't end well.

Take The Quiz!

July 28, 2013

If you answer "NO" to a majority of these questions, then you really have no reason to vote Republican:

Should billionaires be able to bribe politicians via lobbyists?
Should millionaires be able to bank offshore to avoid taxes?
Should US cut food programs for the poor, disabled and elderly?
Should US continue to subsidize corporations making billions?
Should US give tax breaks to corporations outsourcing jobs?
Should state Governments enact laws that are unconstitutional?
Should banks pay less interest on loans than students?
Should bank executives whose actions tanked the economy go free?
Should corporate CEOs pay less percentage of taxes than employees?
Should we ignore all scientific evidence of global warming?
Should US make laws based on religious beliefs of lawmakers?
Should the Senate minority have free reign to stop all legislation?
Should known criminals or domestic abusers be able to buy guns?
Should those with known mental health issues be able to buy guns?
Should peaceful protestors be arrested ignoring the 1st amendment?
Should rallies be allowed with many protestors carrying loaded guns?
Should dangerous industries go unregulated in the name of profit?
Should Congress be allowed to keep submitting the same failed bills?
Should hate speech and be allowed under the 1st amendment?
Should Congress take oaths of allegiance to special interest groups?
Should US give welfare to underpaid employees of billionaires?
Should employers be allowed to fire staff for protesting conditions?
Should legislators be able to pass laws with no public notice or input?
Should the news media be allowed to knowingly tell lies to the public?
Should those with insurance absorb medical costs of those without?
Should schools withhold vital life saving information from students?
Should schools teach religious theories in place of proven science?
Should bills pass that penalize US but monetarily benefit lawmakers?
Should US only subsidize fossil fuel and ignore renewable energy?
Should US allow infrastructure to decay instead of investing in jobs?
Should US prevent working immigrants from a path to citizenship?
Should states be allowed to suppress and obstruct certain voters?
Should US be allowed to spend money citizens contributed into SS?
Should large corporations be absolved of liability for their actions?
Should drug companies be absolved of all liability for their products?
Should sentencing increase to accommodate private prison's quotas?
Should fossil fuel production be allowed to poison drinking water?
Should a GMO food producer be allowed to operate without labeling?
Should any two consenting adults be prevented from marriage?

T-Paw Jokes About Punching A Homeless Woman

August 13, 2013

Former Minnesota Gov and POTUS candidate longshot Tim Pawlenty has been receiving some blowback today for "joking" on Twitter about throwing punches at a homeless woman who was recently [arrested for vandalizing several D.C. landmarks](#), including the Lincoln Memorial.

Here is the tweet:

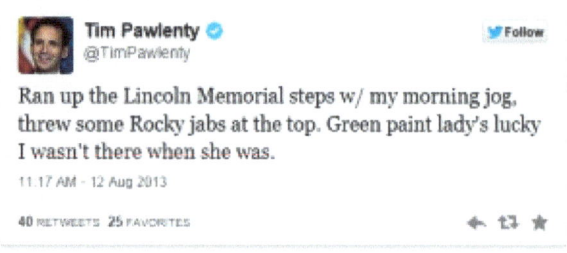

Tim Pawlenty ✔
@TimPawlenty

Ran up the Lincoln Memorial steps w/ my morning jog, threw some Rocky jabs at the top. Green paint lady's lucky I wasn't there when she was.

11:17 AM - 12 Aug 2013

40 RETWEETS 25 FAVORITES

Here is some of the blowback:

Catlin Michael
@CatlinMichael

@TimPawlenty the GOP just keeps killing it with female voters.

11:22 AM - 12 Aug 2013

1 RETWEET 2 FAVORITES

Simon Maloy
@SimonMaloy

That awkward thing where you try to say something patriotic but it comes out as a desire to punch a woman. twitter.com/TimPawlenty/st...

12:02 PM - 12 Aug 2013

14 RETWEETS 9 FAVORITES

I think another thing that is legitimately offensive is Tim Pawlenty trying to be funny. Like, ever. Just stop, T-Paw. You are bad at funny; please stop butchering it. Go back to fishing, or whatever it is you do when you're not busy failing at funny or failing at governing (last I heard it was fishing).

Costa Rica 2013: Costa Rican Beer 101

August 22, 2013

Now that I am back from my vacation I can share with you, in a series of posts, the many things I learned and experienced on my 2nd trip ever to Costa Rica

First up: Beer

Here are the major Costa Rican beers:

Left to Right: Imperial Light, Imperial Silver, Imperial, Rock Ice, Rock Limon, Rock Golden Monkey, Bavaria, Bavaria Dark, Bavaria Silver

Not Pictured: Pilsen

Costa Rica 2013: Two Stamps Are Better Than One

August 22, 2013

Passport stamp:

I like having been to the same far away place in such a short time frame between trips. Made it possible to have the two stamps make it on the same page. Also, you may notice I can check off both international Costa Rican airports from my to-do list and now put them on my "to-do again" list.

Upgraded At Target Field

September 16, 2013

Yesterday my wife and I went to a Twins game at Target Field in Minneapolis. We bought the cheap seats as usual, but then I discovered that using the At the Ballpark app on my phone can allow me to upgrade my seats for a little bit of money. I logged in, put in my ticket seat info, and then it offered me an upgrade from my Section 307 seats (which were $11 seats) to Section 107 for just $9 dollars more per seat!

Here is how that offer turned out:

Here is a panoramic pic... Why the hell not, eh?!?

Pretty sweet, huh... $60 seats for basically $20 each

22 Signs You Might Be A Conservative

September 29, 2013

1: You're irate over the president taking so many vacation days on the taxpayer's dime (92 thus far), but at the same point in Bush's presidency, the 43rd president had spent 367 days at his ranch in Crawford, Texas, and his parent's compound at Kennebunkport, Maine, according to a count by CBS News reporter Mark Knoller.

2: You're happy with your 40 hour work week, paid vacations and company-provided healthcare, but you're strongly anti-union, because those commies haven't done anything for you lately.

3: You strongly support the First Amendment and its guarantee of religious freedom to all, unless the religion is something other than Christianity.

4: You believe Ronald Reagan was a devout Christian, even though he hated going to church, but any president who spends twenty years going to the same Trinity United Church in Chicago must be a Muslim.

5: You believe when a Republican governor creates a healthcare package with an individual mandate for everyone in his state, that's a good idea. But when a Democratic president does it, suddenly it's unconstitutional.

6: You're so enthused about demonstrating your Second Amendment rights, you can think of no finer place to brandish your pistol in public than at a presidential rally.

7: You believe Bill Clinton was responsible for Osama bin Laden's escape ten years ago, but thankfully George W. Bush caught up with him and killed him in Pakistan.

8: You believe in putting American jobs first, except when president Obama rescued 1.5 million GM and Chrysler autoworkers, because that was socialism.

9: It angers you that you can't communicate with the Mexican busboy at your local Olive Garden, but when you took a vacation to San Francisco's Chinatown, you thought it's quaint that so many Chinese-Americans are holding fast to their traditional language. Because that's America!

10: You deny that the lunatic who tried to murder Gaby Giffords was a conservative, even though he targeted a Jewish, pro-choice, pro gay rights, Democratic Congresswoman.

11: You thought it was perfectly normal that every president in history had an untethered right to raise the debt ceiling when warranted, but when Obama asked the GOP held congress to do it, you thought it only natural that it be tied to cutting Social Security and Medicare.

12: When the new 112th Congress was sworn in, you swooned as they promised to focus on "Jobs, jobs, jobs." But when they pivoted, and went after NPR, Planned Parenthood and gay rights, you cheered.

13: You accuse president Obama of raising your taxes to the highest point ever, even though they're lower today than at any time since 1950.

14: You believe the wealthiest Americans are "job creators," and they are — but it doesn't bother you that all the workers in those positions are in India, China and Malaysia, and they're doing the jobs that our fathers once did.

15: You believe gays are anti-American, because their lifestyle is a threat to the children... unless they're married to Tea Party-backed members of Congress from Minnesota.

16: You strongly defend individual freedom, but that freedom doesn't include a woman's right to decide her own healthcare needs.

17: You believe corporations are people too, and are deserving of the same rights as the rest of us. Just not the same obligations to pay personal income tax free of corporate loopholes, or penalties for massive criminal behavior and tax evasion. In these matters, corporations are deserving of special rights.

18: And since corporations are now people too, you must believe in their right to a driver's license, the right to marry, to adopt children, etc. These rights shall not be denied to Exxon, Halliburton and BP (but still immune from the right of the People to try, convict and sentence to death any corporation that conspires to commit a felony... because at that point, they're suddenly not people again.)

19: You still believe Climate Change is a myth, and the recent record highs, lows, floods and droughts around the world coinciding with climate scientist's predictions are all an amazing coincidence. Oh, and Al Gore is FAT!

20: You believe when George W. Bush took the national debt from $5 trillion to $11 trillion, it was necessary for him to do so to keep America safe. But when Barack Obama added to it by trying to rescue the country from a second Great Depression, he was deliberately trying to destroy America!

21: You believe America is a God fearing country, and that the Almighty protects those who believe just as you do. But it's never crossed your mind that the majority of tornadoes, hurricanes and floods all occur in the Bible Belt.

22: You believe that no matter who's in the White House, the office, if not the man himself is deserving of your respect. The only exceptions to this rule, are if his middle name sounds Muslim, and if he's not at least as white as that black guy who works down in the mailroom at the office.

Sometimes I Have To Bust Some Trolls

October 2, 2013

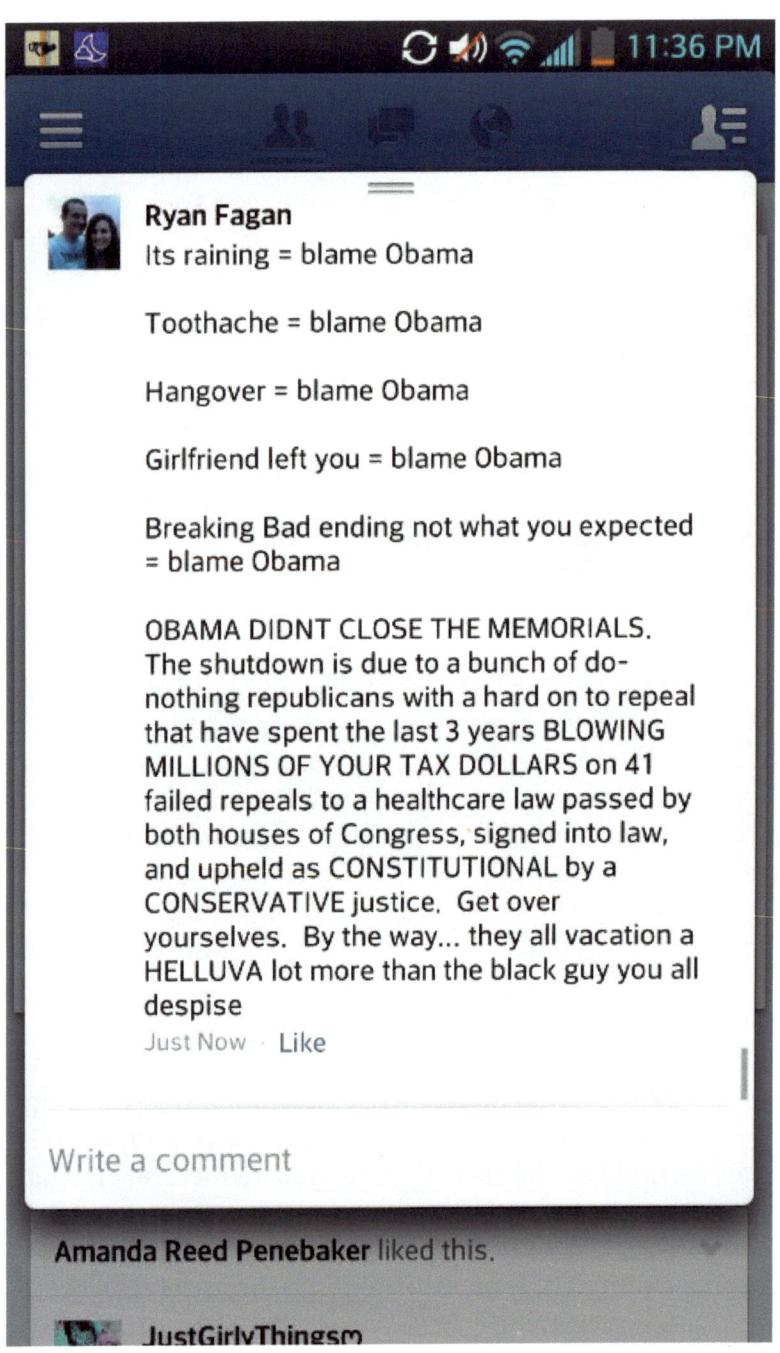

Coming Soon: Worm Burner Golf

October 30, 2013

You An Average Golfer?

www.wormburnergolf.com

Check out the latest golf club
reviews for the average golfer

Worm Burner Golf is launching a full site soon. This is the Google AdWords ad floating around Google now.

A new website is launching soon that will be THE place for average golfers to visit and see the latest golf clubs and equipment get reviewed. Reviews in plain English for the average golfer

How Do You Get The City Of Chicago Convinced That Flu Shots Are Worth It?

November 7, 2013

Put Ditka on a bus.

What You're Really Saying When You Say "Happy Holidays"

November 29, 2013

If the "War on Christmas" was a real thing, Neil deGrasse Tyson won it with an etymology knowledge-bomb.

Happy Holidays is actually an appropriate greeting for this time of year… Always has been (along with Merry Christmas, Happy Hanukkah, etc etc…) and always will be.

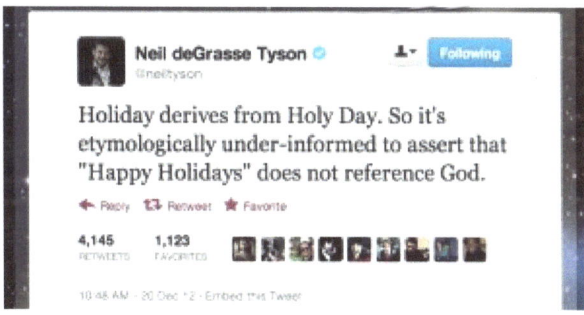

Hey all you "War on Christmas" people… Happy Holidays is actually an appropriate greeting for this time of year!!

The End

For more fun, visit www.faganaround.com